Mahatma Gandhi

Mahatma Gandhi

Caroline Lazo

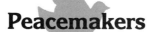

Peacemakers

DILLON PRESS
New York

Maxwell Macmillan Canada
Toronto

Maxwell Macmillan International
New York Oxford Singapore Sydney

To Patty and Peter Evensen

Photo Credits
All photos courtesy of AP-Wide World Photos

Book design by Carol Matsuyama

Library of Congress Cataloging-in Publication Data
Lazo, Caroline Evensen.
  Mahatma Gandhi / by Caroline Lazo. — 1st ed.
    p.   cm. — (Peacemakers)
  Summary: A biography of Mahatma Gandhi, the Indian leader who led his country to freedom from British rule through his policy of nonviolent resistance.
  ISBN 0-87518-526-6
  1. Gandhi, Mahatma, 1869-1948—Juvenile literature. 2. Statesmen—India—Biography—Juvenile literature. 3. Nationalists—India—Biography—Juvenile literature. [1. Gandhi, Mahatma, 1869-1948. 2. Gandhi, Mahatma, 1869-1948. 3. Statesmen.] I. Title. II. Series.
DS481.G3L326   1993
954.03'5'092—dc20   92-14314
[B]

Dillon Press   Maxwell Macmillan Canada, Inc.
Macmillan Publishing Company   1200 Eglinton Avenue East
866 Third Avenue   Suite 200
New York, NY 10022   Don Mills, Ontario M3C 3N1

Macmillan Publishing Company is part of the Maxwell Communication Group of Companies.

First edition

Printed in the United States of America
10 9 8 7 6 5 4 3 2 1

Contents

Introduction

No one would have guessed that a shy little boy like Mohandas Gandhi would one day become the Mahatma ("great soul") of India. Nor would anyone have believed that such a quiet student—who was afraid to speak in class—might someday defeat the British Empire and set his country free. But he did!

Gandhi pursued equal rights for Indians living in South Africa, as well as in India. Without weapons or armies he fought a lifelong battle for India's freedom from British rule. Finally, in 1947, he won. But it was the modest way he lived—the way he practiced what he preached—that won the hearts of millions. Writers and photographers from the richest nations in the world traveled to India to talk with Gandhi. They watched him at his spinning wheel and walked with him on the beach, listening carefully as he spoke about his commitment to peace. Through their stories and pictures Gandhi's search for truth and peace became known throughout the world. And when an assassin's bullet killed him on January 30, 1948, the whole world mourned. Hundreds of thousands of people—kings and laborers alike—joined the funeral procession in Delhi the next day. Great leaders eulogized

Gandhi speaks to a gathering of the Indian Congress Party.

him and compared him to Buddha and to Christ.

Such praise might have embarrassed Mahatma Gandhi. When people called him a saint—and even a god—he usually cringed. "Often the title [Mahatma] has deeply pained me," he wrote in his autobiography. He believed he had too many faults and fears to deserve that awesome name.

Sometimes he joked about people's godlike view of him. Once, for example, a man riding with him on a train

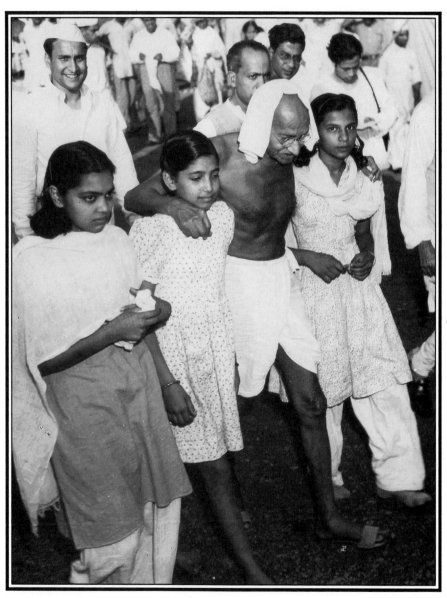

Gandhi walks through the streets supported by one of his granddaughters and her friend.

fell off the platform but survived unharmed. He told Gandhi he had escaped injury because he had been sitting next to a saint. Gandhi replied, "If that were true, you should not have fallen at all!"

Though Gandhi's childhood gave no clues to his future greatness, his mother's self-discipline and devotion to her religion set a lasting example for her son. Her willingness to sacrifice in order to keep her vows deeply impressed Gandhi as a child—and inspired him in his quest for peace later on.

"If we are to reach real peace," he wrote, "we shall have to begin with children."

A Nation in Chains

In 1869, the year Mohandas Gandhi was born, India was ruled by Great Britain—just as America had been a century before. To win their freedom, Americans used every available weapon—from rifles to cannon fire—and defeated the British forces. Farms became battlefields, and thousands lost their lives.

The American Revolution was like a warning to kings and conquerors everywhere—people wanted to choose their own leaders and were willing to die for the right to do so. But "the shot heard 'round the world" was barely audible in India, where the people were weary from centuries of bloody battles started by foreign leaders who wanted to rule them.

Since the 1600s, Great Britain, France, Portugal, and other European countries had fought over India because of its rich supply of tea, spices, indigo (used to make blue dye for ink), textiles, and other goods. Products made in Great Britain from these resources were then sold back to India at a high cost to the Indian people. The British became richer that way, while the majority of Indians lived in poverty.

In those days ships carrying supplies across the oceans were often raided by pirates and lost at sea. For this reason, many countries were hesitant to attempt trading with the far ports of India. But the British East India Company—with help from the British government—finally managed to stop the piracy. In 1858 it took control of

India's seaports and, as a result, the country itself.

The Indian people were too poor and weak from hunger to consider waging war against the British, as the Americans had done. Tough questions would always stop them: Even if they were strong enough, who would dare to lead them? Who could possibly unify 200 million people who lived in hundreds of separate states and spoke hundreds of different languages? Unarmed and unskilled, what chance would they have in a war against the awesome British Empire—the strongest military power on earth?

Feeling doomed, many turned to their religion—to Hindu gods such as Vishnu, Brahma, and Shiva—in hopes of finding some freedom and peace of mind. Yet, at the same time, they had no choice but to accept their roles as servants or slaves of the powerful British lords who ruled them.

"We did not conquer India for the benefit of the Indians," Lord Brentford wrote. "We conquered India as the outlet for the goods of Great Britain . . . and by the sword we will hold it."

Then came Gandhi.

Family and Friends

Mohandas Karamchand Gandhi was born on October 2, 1869, in Porbander, on the northwest coast of India. Today Porbander is a part of Gujarat, a larger state, but in Gandhi's time it was a state of its own. Mohandas's father, Karamchand Gandhi, was the *diwan* (prime minister or chief aide) to the prince in power there. Indian royal families were allowed to maintain their rule in some states as long as they—and all their subjects—remained loyal to the British Empire. "My father was a Diwan," Gandhi wrote later, "but nevertheless a servant."

Though the name Gandhi means "grocer" in the Gujartai language, the Gandhi men had been diwans for three generations, and both Karamchand and his wife, Putlibai Gandhi, expected one of their three sons to follow the tradition. Mohandas, his two brothers and sister were devoted to their parents. Their father was well-known in Porbander and neighboring states for his fairness and integrity. But it was their mother, a devout Hindu, whose gentle manner, kindness, and cheerful attitude—even in troubled times—young Mohandas admired more than anyone.

"The outstanding impression my mother has left on

Mohandas Gandhi (right) with his brother Laxmidas in 1886, when he was 17.

my memory," he wrote years later, "is that of saintliness. . . . She would take the hardest vows and keep them without flinching."

Putlibai was Karamchand's fourth wife. His previous wives had died. With two daughters from those marriages and three sons and a daughter from his marriage to Putlibai, the Gandhi household was a lively one! And the family shared their large three-story house with Karamchand Gandhi's five brothers and their families, too. So Mohandas grew up with people of all ages and always had someone at home to play with.

When any of the Gandhi children became ill, Mohandas's mother sat with them—nieces, nephews, and her own children alike—and nursed them until they were well again. She loved them all, and Mohandas would always remember that.

Mohandas was much happier at home than at school. He was extremely shy in class, and his books became his best companions. Because he was smaller than others his age and self-conscious about his large ears, he avoided making friends and would run straight home after school. "I literally ran back, because I could not bear to talk to

The Gandhi house in Rajkot

anybody," he recalled later. "I was even afraid lest anyone should poke fun at me."

Mohandas had difficulty with the multiplication tables in the early grades, and he called himself a "mediocre" student. He liked to read in school, but the stories his mother told him at home were the ones he enjoyed the most.

Hindu Customs

After school, the Gandhi children would often gather in the courtyard in front of their house. Mrs. Gandhi would join them and tell them tales of Hindu gods who saved the earth from evil forces. The story of Vishnu and the sea demons was a favorite:

> While demons busily churned the ocean of eternity— hoping to find the secret to eternal life—strange objects rose to the surface. One of them was the earth in the form of a goddess. The multi- coiled demon king quickly pulled her down to the bottom of the sea. Then Vishnu, god of preservation, turned into Varaha, a cosmic savior, and plunged to the ocean floor to rescue the goddess. He crushed the demon's coils under his foot and carefully lifted the goddess (earth) up to safety among the gods.

Hindu society is divided into castes, and because the earliest Gandhis were grocers, Mohandas's parents belonged to the merchant caste. At that time, each caste included a specific group of people: *Brahmans* (priests); *Kshatriyas* (civic and military leaders); *Vaisyas* (merchants); and *Shudras* (craftsmen). Below all of these castes were the outcastes—the Untouchables—who were called "unclean" because of their dirty, lowly work. When Mohandas grew older, he called these people *harijans* ("children of God") and brought an end to the prejudice against them.

Though Putlibai Gandhi could neither read nor write, she was highly intelligent and deeply religious. "She would not think of taking her meals without her daily prayers," her son recalled later. And she never missed the *Chaturmas*, the period of fasting during the four-month-long rainy season. Acts of self-sacrifice and self-discipline helped to prepare her, she believed, for her reincarnation, or rebirth, in the next life.

To the Hindus (there are about 400 million in and around India today) all forms of life command respect. For that reason, the Gandhis vowed never to eat the meat of any animal and expected their children to do the same.

A visit to *Haveli,* the Vaishnava temple, was a daily duty for Putlibai Gandhi; and Mohandas often went with her, though he was never comfortable there. The temple, he thought, was too formal and fancy. But the annual New

Year festival of *Diwali* was different. It was fun from beginning to end.

During Diwali relatives would come together and exchange gifts, as Christians do on Christmas and Jews during Hanukkah. But the magic came at night when Hindus lit tiny lamps of oil and put them on their doorsteps and along the streets, where the lamps flickered like candles throughout the night.

When Mohandas grew up, he remembered the "spirit of joy" that pervaded the holidays when he was a boy.

High-School Years

By the time Mohandas entered high school, the Gandhis had moved to the neighboring state of Rajkot, where, again, his father was the diwan. Though the family wasn't wealthy, they lived comfortably and employed a nurse named Rambha to help raise the children. She was like a member of the family and taught Mohandas how to face his shyness and fears.

"I used to be haunted by the fear of thieves, ghosts, and serpents," he confessed. "I could not bear to sleep without a light in the room." He was embarrassed to admit to such fears in high school, but Rambha gave him good advice: By repeating a sacred text (*mantra*) whenever he became afraid, he would clear his mind and overcome the fear. To his surprise, the early advice—and his mantra *Ramanama*—helped him through some of his toughest trials in later life.

Mohandas studied hard in high school, because his teachers expected him to. He had been taught to respect his elders and was afraid to disappoint them. But the book that influenced him the most during his first year in high school was found at home. It was the story of the Hindu hero Shravana, who carried his blind parents in slings over his shoulders on a religious pilgrimage. Such devotion to one's parents moved Mohandas to tears, and he decided to try to model himself after Shravana.

During that same year he saw the play *Harishchandra,* which was about a king who gave up everything in order to gain truth. Mohandas was haunted by one question: "Why should not all be truthful like Harishchandra?" "To follow Truth . . . and to go through all the ordeals . . . inspired me," he wrote in his autobiography.

Certain events in school also helped to shape his future. One time, the educational inspector visited his class and gave a spelling test. The teacher noticed that Mohandas had misspelled a word and gently kicked his foot to get his attention. Then he motioned to Mohandas to copy his neighbor's answer, because he wanted his class to impress the inspector with a perfect score. Though Mohandas respected his teacher, he respected the truth even more. So he refused to copy his neighbor's test and later received harsh criticism from his teacher. But the event never changed his respect for his teacher. Later he explained why: "I was by nature blind to the faults of elders."

When he was only 13 years old, Mohandas was told he would marry Kasturbai Makanji, a girl his own age, from Porbandar. Childhood marriage was an old tradition in India; parents started planning it when their children were only six or seven years old. At the time, Mohandas

Gandhi with his wife, Kasturbai

never questioned his parents' decision, but many years later he blamed his father for following such an old-fashioned custom and for making him marry so young. "It was preposterously early!" he said.

If children were still in school when they were married, they continued to live at their respective homes. And sometimes Kasturbai lived with her parents, and Mohandas with his. Though Mohandas was devoted to his wife, he soon became jealous, and insisted that she ask his permission before leaving the house. Wives were expected to obey their husbands. But Kasturbai was independent, and she finally helped him realize that his restrictions were unfair. She won him over to her point of view. And Mohandas learned an early lesson in the power of love and logic to change one's way of thinking. If he could be persuaded to see his errors, so could others, he thought. And many years later he would put his own theory of nonviolent persuasion into action—and change the minds of an entire nation.

Mohandas had grown used to the presence of British officials in Porbandar and Rajkot. Those he met through his father were decent people. It was his faith in the basic decency of the British that would convince him that their minds could be changed someday, and that India could be a partner of Great Britain instead of its servant. But other challenges would come first.

Early Challenges

Mohandas made new friends in high school, though he was still shy and self-conscious about his small size. One friend, a Muslim boy, explained that by eating meat Mohandas would become bigger and stronger. "We [Indians] are a weak people," he told Mohandas, "because we do not eat meat. The English are able to rule over us, because they are meat eaters." His view echoed a popular poem in circulation around the school.

> Behold the mighty Englishman
> He rules the Indian small
> Because being a meat eater
> He is five cubits tall.

Mohandas had been told that his new friend was not an honorable person, but Mohandas thought he could reform him. Besides, his friend was strong and could run long distances at great speed. "I was dazzled by this friend's exploits," he wrote. "I could hardly jump or run. Why should I not also be as strong as he?"

Afraid that his parents would be "shocked to death" by his plan to break their rules, Mohandas met his friend at a secret place by a nearby river to taste the forbidden meat. But he still believed he was following the Truth because he planned to reform his friend.

More meat-eating sessions followed until Mohandas felt too sick to continue the procedure. Also, he felt guilty when he had to explain his loss of appetite to his parents. Nightmares began to haunt him. At the same time, one of his cousins encouraged Mohandas to steal pennies from the servants and a gold coin from his brother. Soon his conscience bothered him so much he could stand it no longer, and he and his cousin decided to commit suicide by eating a poisonous plant! But they quickly realized that such an act would only hurt their parents much more. So Mohandas wrote a confession and gave it to his father.

When Karamchand Gandhi read his son's words, he was so proud of Mohandas's courage to tell the truth that he forgave everything he had done. As a result, they became closer than ever before. And when his father became ill, Mohandas ran home after school every day to be with him. He massaged his father's legs and took care of him until late at night, giving his mother a chance to rest.

Mohandas's wife, Kasturbai, was pregnant when Karamchand was sick, so Mohandas needed to be with her, too. But one night, after leaving his father to return to Kasturbai, his father died. Mohandas was overcome with sorrow and guilt. "It is a blot I have never been able to efface or forget," he wrote later.

The tragedy awakened a new sense of responsibility in Mohandas—a desire to study hard and to put an end to the temptations of his teenage years.

Gandhi as a law student in England

Law School in London

Mohandas's father had hoped that his son would follow the family tradition and become a diwan. Above all, he had wanted his son to be well educated. But after Karamchand died, there was little money for college education or for anything else. "My father never had any ambition to accumulate riches," Mohandas wrote later. Yet money wasn't the only barrier that seemed to block his way to college. His mother's fears and ancient Hindu vows confronted him, too.

After an unhappy term at Samaldas College in Bhavnagar, Mohandas decided to take the advice of an old family friend and try to go to college in London. The idea of living in London—the capital of the British Empire—fascinated Mohandas. "What better way to learn the English language, laws, and traditions than to live right there—in England?" he asked himself. And if he hoped to improve life in local Indian towns someday, he thought he should learn as much as possible about the British who ruled over them. But Mohandas's mother was afraid to let her son travel thousands of miles to England. "Someone had told her," he wrote, "that young men took to meat, and could not live there without liquor."

Mohandas reassured his mother and vowed not to touch meat, wine, or women while in England. And his older brother arranged to pay his expenses so he could enroll in the law school of the Inner Temple in London. Finally, on September 4, 1888, Mohandas said good-bye to his mother, his wife, and their baby son and sailed for England.

He was uncomfortable on board ship, because he knew little English and was not familiar with the Western food he was served or the style of clothes people wore. When he arrived in London, he felt self-conscious in his white flannel suit; everyone seemed to stare at him. But he soon adapted to the new city life and bought expensive suits and took ballroom-dancing lessons to become more like the Englishmen he met. One friend, Dr. P. J. Mehta, advised him on English manners as well: "Do not ask questions as we usually do in India on first acquaintance; never address people as 'sir' while speaking to them as we do in India; only servants and subordinates address their masters that way."

Gandhi soon tired of the rich food served at parties and the fancy clothes he had bought. And he felt it was unfair to his brother who was paying his expenses. So he changed his way of life; he walked miles to save bus fare, moved to a smaller room, and kept careful track of the money he spent. He discovered a vegetarian restaurant where at last he found the kind of food he loved—fruits, vegetables, and his favorite dates and nuts. He became a member of the Executive Committee of the Vegetarian Society and began to write articles for its journal. "I had not the courage to speak and I therefore set down my thoughts in writing," he later recalled.

Gandhi met a variety of friends in the Vegetarian Society—including Hindus and Christians—and became interested in various religions. He read the Bhagavad Gita, the Hindu sacred text. "I regard it today as the book par excellence for the knowledge of Truth," he said. But he also found "the highest form of religion in the Bible's New Testament—especially The Sermon on the Mount, which, he said, "went straight to my heart." His basic philosophy is summed up in the New Testament as well:

> Be not overcome of evil,
> but overcome evil with good.

Gandhi followed no one religious text because he found valuable truths in many religions. He told his friend, author Louis Fischer, "I am a Christian and a Hindu and a Muslim and a Jew." To Gandhi, God was Truth. But he respected the views of others and always wanted to hear them.

In June 1891, Gandhi passed his law exams in London and sailed back home to India—and to a special assignment that would alter the course of his life.

Turning Points

When Gandhi arrived home, he was told that his mother had died. Though filled with sorrow, he was determined to honor her memory by working hard and following the Truth as she had done. His wife seemed to know that his work would take him away from her again but would bring him back again, too. He didn't want to leave her and their

Gandhi outside his law office in South Africa in 1900

two sons, Harilal and Manilal, but in 1893 he was offered a one-year job in South Africa he couldn't resist.

The thought of working in South Africa excited Gandhi. More than 90,000 Indians lived there, and he was sure he would feel at home. Like India, South Africa was a part of the British Empire, ruled by British lords. Gandhi had more self-confidence after his college years in London and had now mastered the English language. So the thought of working under British domination didn't bother him. Most important, he had studied English law and could recite historic cases at the drop of a hat. But to his surprise, it was his hat that caused his first clash in the South African courts!

When Gandhi walked into the courtroom in Durban, South Africa, he was wearing a turban on his head—a typical Indian headdress. He was told to remove it at once. Gandhi refused and left the court. Later, he changed his mind and wore no hat at all, because he knew he had a better chance to change such rules if he played by the rules—at least in the beginning. He had also been advised by his law firm, Dada Abdulla & Co., not to wear an English hat "because you will pass for a waiter." Indians

Wearing traditional Indian clothing, Gandhi attends a conference in London.

in South Africa, he soon discovered, were classified into many groups and were prisoners of prejudice.

The majority of Indians in South Africa belonged to the laboring class. The British called them "coolies," or *samis,* and other insulting names. Gandhi enjoyed reminding the British that in the Sanskrit language, *sami* meant "master"! "Some Englishmen would wince at this," he wrote, "while others would get angry and swear."

When Gandhi was asked to attend a business meeting in Pretoria, he had no idea that the trip would be the major turning point in his life. He had been warned that there was even more prejudice against Indians in Pretoria than in Durban. But Gandhi accepted the challenge because, after all, he was a lawyer working for a distinguished law firm. Such a position would be respected anywhere, he thought. So he dressed according to the rules—in a dark business suit—and boarded the train for Pretoria.

With his first-class ticket in hand, Gandhi went directly to his compartment and started to read a book as the train left the station. Soon, British officials informed him that he was not allowed to sit in the first-class section; Indians were forbidden to ride there, whether or not they had the proper tickets. Gandhi refused to move to the baggage section, where they said he belonged. So the officials pushed and kicked him off the train.

Shivering from the cold, he sat alone in the train station and wondered what to do next. In his autobiography he recalled the questions that plagued him at that crucial moment in his life:

Should I fight for my rights or go back to India, or should I go on to Pretoria without minding the insults?. . . It would be cowardice to run back to India without fulfilling my obligation. The hardship to which I was subjected was superficial—only a symptom of the deep disease of colour prejudice. I should try, if possible, to root out the disease and suffer hardships in the process.

Gandhi sent a telegram to his law firm in Durban to tell them about his experience on the train, and the lawyers arranged for his safe trip to Pretoria. Yet, while riding in a stagecoach during part of his travel, he was called a sami and told to ride outside on the footboard. When he refused to obey, he was beaten. And when he tried to stay at a hotel, he was told there was "no room," and he knew why.

Gandhi received praise for his work in the law firm, but he decided to use his talent and knowledge to help the Indian people achieve their human rights. He began by filing a petition against the state government in Natal when it proposed to end the Indians' right to vote. London accepted the petition and turned down the Natal proposal. But the unfair law passed in South Africa!

Gandhi knew that the road to equality for the Indians

would be long and difficult. Yet he was determined to make changes that would last. To do so, he would have to change the thinking of the white people in South Africa and the British throughout the empire. Gandhi knew that harmony could only happen when all people were treated equally, and he was willing to devote the rest of his life to that principle. But he knew he couldn't do it alone; he would have to inspire the Indian people to help him.

Steps to Freedom

By 1894 Indians in South Africa had begun to listen—and love—their new leader. He organized the Natal Indian Congress to benefit the Indian community in its struggle for better schools and living conditions and fair treatment in general. News of Gandhi's work spread to villages throughout the country, where many thousands of illiterate Indians praised his work and wanted to help him.

But Gandhi missed his wife and children, so he returned to India. He wrote articles about the terrible

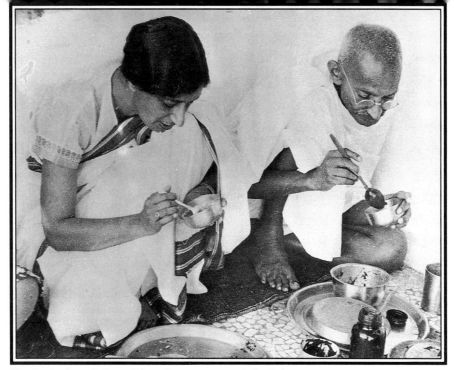

Kasturbai and Gandhi eating supper at their home.

treatment Indians received in South Africa, and he began to win support from Indians at home. Though he had finished his one-year assignment in South Africa, he had much unfinished work to do there. So once again he decided to leave India—this time, with his wife and children—and return to Durban, where new challenges were waiting.

When the Boers, Dutch farmers in South Africa, waged war against the British, Gandhi advised his followers to support the British. He explained his stand this way.

> I felt that, if I demanded rights as a British citizen, it was also my duty, as such, to participate in the defense of the British Empire.

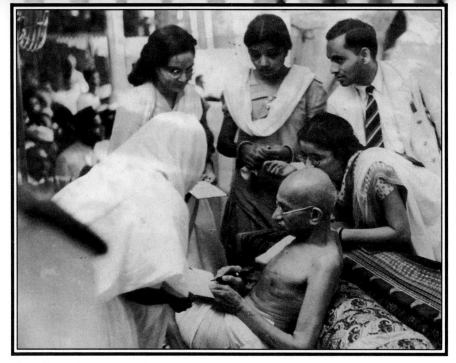

Gandhi sells autographs to raise money to support his cause.

Opposed to violence, Gandhi and his supporters enlisted as ambulance workers, and they eventually earned the war medal for their outstanding service. Newspapers featured stories about them, "and the Indians' prestige was enhanced," Gandhi said.

In 1903 Gandhi published his newsletter, *Indian Opinion*. Its pages carried his message—equal rights for Indians—to thousands of his countrymen living in South Africa. Without modern means of communication, Gandhi was never sure how many would show up for a scheduled protest or community meeting. The huge crowds that came wherever he appeared often brought tears to his eyes. "He always smiled as he greeted them," one reporter noted. "He didn't even have to speak. He radiated such power and goodness that his presence alone made them feel strong." And they called him "Bapu" (father).

When Indians were ordered to carry a special identification pass—or go to prison if they did not obey—Gandhi refused to comply. He put his principle of *satyagraha* into action. *Sat*, meaning "truth," and *agraha*, meaning "firmness," his unique principle of peaceful force was born. Called "soul force," it inspired people to resist unfair laws by not cooperating with them in a nonviolent way.

Gandhi later explained the logic behind the principle to historian William L. Shirer:

> The British want us to put the struggle on the plane of machine guns, where they have the weapons and we do not. Our only assurance of beating them is putting the struggle on a plane where we have the weapons and they have not.

Believing that truth was firmly on their side, Gandhi and his followers were willing to be imprisoned for refusing to obey unjust laws. In fact, they *wanted* to be jailed to show how deeply they believed in their cause. (Years later Martin

Luther King would call himself "a disciple of Gandhi.")

In 1908 Gandhi went to London to try to gain some support for the Indians' plight in South Africa. But when he returned, he was imprisoned for failing to register for the identification pass. He was freed when South African general Jan Christiaan Smuts promised to revoke the ID law if the Indians would register, which they did. But Smuts broke his promise and kept the unfair law in force. In response, Gandhi organized a quiet, mass burning of the registration cards. Others refused to register at all. Many were beaten, and thousands went to jail.

Gandhi was jailed again when he protested the law that legalized Christian marriages only. Hindu and Muslim marriages (Indian marriages) were illegal, according to South African law—including his own!

While in prison, Gandhi read the works of Leo Tolstoy, Ralph Waldo Emerson, and Henry David Thoreau. He called Thoreau's essay "Civil Disobedience" a "mastery treatise." He admired Tolstoy's goal to create harmony between his religious beliefs and everyday activities. And when Gandhi was released from prison, he established Tolstoy Farm, where he pursued the same kind of

Gandhi sits quietly by his spinning wheel on his farm.

harmony. At Tolstoy, Indian families worked together to develop their skills, grow their own food, and make their own clothes. Gandhi, wearing a simple *dhoti* (loin cloth), spent much of the day at his spinning wheel. He practiced what he preached. Children, including his own, learned from their elders' examples. They learned best, Gandhi said, when taught "cheerfully."

After visiting Gandhi at Tolstoy Farm, Indian nationalist Gopal Gokhale told friends about Gandhi's special talent: "Gandhi has the marvelous spiritual power to turn ordinary men around him into heroes."

Gandhi's dedication to satyagraha and his ability to bring out the best in people finally met success in South Africa. General Smuts came around to Gandhi's point of view and agreed to his most important demands. And in 1914 a new law that gave Indians their basic rights as citizens of South Africa was passed.

Though the new law was not perfect, Gandhi was satisfied with the giant steps Indians had taken to improve their life in South Africa. So in 1915 he and his family, including two more sons, sailed back to India, where millions of people lived in poverty under British law.

Road to Independence

When Gandhi arrived in Bombay, crowds of Indians gathered to greet him. He was a hero. Like Vishnu, he had conquered the demons of destruction and had returned safely home. But as he traveled around India, he saw poverty, unfair laws, bad working conditions, and prejudice against the Untouchables, because, like janitors, they had the dirtiest jobs. Gandhi was glad to be home, but he saw hard work ahead.

He gave away his business suits and wore only Indian clothing—including his favorite turban. And instead of English, he spoke his native Gujarati language. Indians surrounded him wherever he went and listened to his advice. Even those living in the remotest villages knew who he was: he was one of them.

Rabindranath Tagore, the famous Indian poet, called him "Mahatma," meaning "great soul" or "saint." But Gandhi wasn't comfortable with the title, because he had broken vows in the past and he felt "too far from perfection" to deserve it. Others disagreed, and soon the whole world began to call him Mahatma Gandhi.

Gandhi and his family started an *ashram*, a commune similar to Tolstoy Farm, where they practiced the

principles of equality and nonviolence. He invited a family of Untouchables to live there, too, though Kasturbai opposed it. Gandhi was determined to change the Hindu caste system, which forbade contact with Untouchables. His bold move to include them in the ashram was another example of practicing what he preached—equal rights for all Indians.

When nearby mill workers complained about their bad working conditions, Gandhi urged them to strike. But they were afraid. Gandhi believed he had failed to inspire them, so he started his first public fast. He refused to eat any food until the workers were ready to strike for fair wages and safe conditions. Then the workers rallied, and the mill owners met their demands. "Goodwill was created all around," Gandhi wrote. His goal was always harmony. When there are winners and losers, he said, there is often some lasting tension and unhappiness.

The road to fair government in India got rougher, and goodwill was hard to find. But Gandhi didn't give up. He supported the British in World War I (1914-1918) because he believed such loyalty would produce home rule (locally elected government) in India. But after the war, the

Surrounded by followers, Gandhi spreads his message of nonviolence.

British gave Gandhi no such reward. Indian home rule was refused. Gandhi called a strike.

When Gandhi was arrested, some Indians turned to violence against the British. Again, Gandhi fasted for three days, because he believed he had failed to teach those Indians the true meaning of satyagraha and nonviolence. But on April 13, 1919, Gandhi's hope for harmony with the British in India was crushed.

While 15,000 Indians gathered in a square at Amritsar for a peaceful celebration of the New Year, British General Reginald Dyer's troops opened fire on the unarmed crowd. More than 400 Indians were killed and 11,000 wounded. The British, Gandhi said, no longer had a right to rule India. But home rule, even if granted, would not be enough. From then on, India's total independence from the British Empire would be his goal.

The Fearless Mahatma

Strike by strike, more Indians found the courage to defend their rights—and to suffer, if necessary, in the process. Gandhi continued to gain strength from reading the Bhagavad Gita and from practicing the Hindu principles of *aparigraha* (absence of possessions) and *samabhava* (equal acceptance of pain or pleasure, defeat or victory). Without material possessions or desires to distract him, he could focus totally on his goal—India's freedom from foreign rule. Nothing could stop him. He was fearless.

As head of the Indian National Congress, Gandhi called for more strikes against unfair taxes and bad working conditions, as well as all-out boycotts of British products. He inspired millions of Indians to spin their own cloth rather than pay high prices for materials imported from England. Spinning became a symbol of Indian independence. Though officials in London were outraged, they began to see that Gandhi, like a strong wind, was gaining momentum and could not be controlled—not even in prison: "I renewed my energy there," he said.

By 1922 more than 35,000 people had been imprisoned in India for defying British laws. But the most massive protest—involving 100,000 people—made head-

Gandhi arrives in London to discuss the future of India with
British leaders.

lines from Bombay to Boston. It was Gandhi's 200-mile-long march to the sea at Dandi, where he picked up a handful of salt from the shore. Indians weren't allowed to touch the salt along its coasts, because it was taxed by the British, and only the British could take it from the sea. So Gandhi's bold action at once defied the law and swelled the tide of support for India's independence.

Though thousands, including Gandhi, were put in prison, the Salt March was Gandhi's most successful and symbolic act. It was India's own "shot heard 'round the world"—especially in London. There, the British leaders recalled the Boston Tea Party, when Americans rebelled against the British tax on tea by dumping a whole cargo into the harbor.

Gandhi's goal was not to hurt the British but to change their view of India.

> My ambition is no less than to convert the British people through nonviolence, and thus make them see the wrong they have done to India.

The British finally gave in to Gandhi and allowed Indians to distill the salt from their shores. And when the marchers were freed from prison, they held a convention of the All-India Congress. They resolved to win total independence for India and the right to withdraw from the British Empire. The next year, 1931, Gandhi was asked to represent the Congress at the Round Table Conference in London—and to meet the king of England.

Gandhi's youngest son, Devadas, served as his secretary and would join his father on that historic trip in September 1931. His other sons, Harilal, Manilal, and Ramdas, saw very little of their father, which Gandhi regretted. But as he explained to a reporter: "All of India is my family now."

"Man of the Year"

Writers, reporters, photographers—all the media—loved Mahatma Gandhi. They scrambled to be near him; they didn't want to miss a word he said. He spoke softly and "was always so kind and patient with us," one reporter

Gandhi surrounded by British supporters during his 1931 trip to England.

said. In London from September 12 through December 5, 1931, they followed him closely and reported his efforts to win India's freedom from the British Empire.

While Gandhi had tea with King George V, reporters waited patiently outside Buckingham Palace. When the doors finally opened, there stood Gandhi—dressed in his usual loincloth, homespun shawl, and sandals.

"Were you comfortable in such light clothing, sir?" one reporter asked.

"Do not worry," Gandhi replied. "The king wore enough for both of us!"

In *Gandhi: A Memoir*, William Shirer described his interviews with Gandhi:

To observe firsthand that mighty effort . . . the towering greatness, the goodness, the humor, the humility, the integrity and purity of purpose, and that indefinable thing, the genius, of this man was the greatest stroke of fortune that ever befell me.

Only the British were surprised when *Time* magazine selected Gandhi for its "Man of the Year" in January 1931. Journalist Henry Brailsford covered the story:

In India I saw what no one is likely to see again. Bombay obeyed two governments—the British with all its power . . . and one of its prisoners: Mahatma Gandhi.

Brailsford condemned the "cold English brains" that allowed Indian men and women to be kicked and beaten while peacefully protesting unfair laws. He noted that even with bruised arms and swollen faces, they walked tall down the streets of Bombay because Gandhi had given them courage.

World praise and publicity attracted millions to Gandhi's cause—but aroused only more frustration among

British officials. They didn't dare hurt Gandhi because they feared all of India might go on strike. He had become so loved that when he was jailed, Indians refused to pay any taxes until he was freed.

After the meetings in London in 1931, Gandhi returned to India—without the promise of independence he had hoped for. But, as he told William Shirer, "I am always optimistic. I admit I do not see land in sight yet. But neither did Columbus, so it is said, until the last moment."

Into Indian Hands

In the years following the Round Table Conference in London, Gandhi traveled throughout India and spoke about satyagraha and human rights, including equality for women. He was imprisoned while campaigning for the rights of the Untouchables—the harijans—but finally, after a long fast, won their freedom. From then on, they could enjoy the same activities as other Hindus. That was a major victory for Gandhi, because even as a little boy he wanted to see them treated fairly.

When World War II began, Britain expected India's support. But without a promise of independence, the Indian people said no. Gandhi led new protests against the British. He and his friend Jawaharlal Nehru—India's future and first prime minister—were imprisoned along with 100,000 others. "Quit India!" became more than a slogan throughout the country; it became the demand of millions of Indians.

But the British remained steadfast. If they freed India, they would lose income, cheap labor and, above all, a major part of its empire. Just the thought of the loss was too much for British prime minister Winston Churchill: "I have not become the king's first minister," he said, "in order to preside at the liquidation of the British Empire."

Gandhi fasted in prison, and his wife joined him there. Kasturbia's health worsened, and in 1942 she died. Grief stricken, Gandhi was released.

A few years later, after the war ended in Europe, Clement R. Attlee became Britain's new prime minister. Unlike Churchill, Attlee agreed with Gandhi that India should be free. And on February 18, 1947, he made this historic announcement:

> His Majesty's government wish to make it clear that it is their definite intention . . . to effect the transference of power into Indian hands by a date not later than June 1948.

At last, Indian independence was assured.

Just as India and Great Britain were about to make peace, Hindus and Muslims began to fight each other! Some Muslims felt overwhelmed by the large Hindu majority in India and demanded a state of their own. Though Gandhi always wanted a united India, on August 14, 1947, he agreed to the plan that made Pakistan a separate country for Muslims.

The next day, August 15, 1947, India's freedom from the British Empire was legally granted. Lord Louis Mountbatten, India's last British viceroy, relinquished his power. But Gandhi did not attend the Independence Day ceremony. He was more comfortable at home, where he could fast and pray in silence. Nearly 78 years old, he was growing weak and tired. And as long as some of his people were killing each other, his work was not done. He could not recall any time in his life when Hindus and Muslims fought each other. Many believed the strife was caused by overcrowded cities and confusion along the new borders. But Gandhi felt he had failed to teach Muslim leader Mohammed Ali Jinnah—and other extremists—the principles of peace and brotherhood.

Against doctors' orders, Gandhi visited areas where violence was rampant and pacified many of the uprisings. But some were too dangerous to walk into, so, in Delhi Gandhi used his most powerful weapon—a "fast unto death"—to restore peace. He refused to touch food until the Muslim and Hindu leaders came to him to declare an end to all the fighting in India.

By the third day, leaders and followers alike from all over the country arrived in Delhi to make sure Gandhi didn't die. They were shocked to see how weak he was, his voice barely above a whisper. They called him "Bapu" and said prayers for him—Hindus and Muslims together, also Sikhs, Christians, and Jews.

After their declaration of peace was signed, the violence ended. News of the successful fast spread around

Too weak to walk after his fast to end the fighting between Hindus and Muslims, Gandhi is carried out to greet the crowds.

the world. At the United Nations in New York, the Pakistani foreign minister said, "A new and tremendous wave of feeling and desire for friendship . . . is sweeping the subcontinent in response to the fast."

January 30, 1948

Gandhi regained his strength while staying with his good friend G. D. Birla near Delhi. The beautiful lawns surrounding the Birla house provided a peaceful setting for afternoon prayer meetings. Though stone walls guarded the estate, extra police protection was offered to Gandhi because of the recent violence in the area. But Gandhi refused it. He was not afraid.

On January 30, 1948, flanked by friends and loyal aides, Gandhi walked outside to greet the crowd and to lead them in prayer. As he walked toward the platform, people moved aside, some bowing to him as he passed. But one man—a Hindu fanatic who blamed Gandhi for making peace with the Muslims—was in the crowd, too. He edged his way through until he came face to face with Gandhi. Looking straight at him, he aimed his pistol and fired three shots. Gandhi died instantly in the arms of his aides.

The assassin, Nathuram Godse, was captured and later tried and sentenced to death. But Gandhi's sons knew their father would have opposed a death sentence, because he had opposed *all* killing. In spite of their pleas for a prison term instead, Godse was hanged.

Covered with rose petals, the body of Mahatma Gandhi lies in state after his assassination.

"I cannot intentionally hurt anything that lives," Gandhi wrote in 1930, "much less human beings, even though they may do the greatest wrong to me."

The Last March

No street in Delhi was wide enough to hold the 400,000 people who marched in Gandhi's funeral procession on January 31. They spread to the banks of the Jamuna River, and they perched in trees and on rooftops to say farewell to their leader as his bier passed by.

Gandhi's murder was felt in every corner of the world. The United Nations flag was lowered to half-mast as members spoke about his lifelong work for peace. In London, Lord Louis Montbatten said, "Mahatma Gandhi will go down in history with Buddha and Christ." Albert Einstein said:

> Generations to come will scarce believe that such a one as this ever in flesh and blood walked upon this earth.

All across India people lit candles and said prayers as they thought of the quiet, courageous man who devoted his life to winning their freedom—not with weapons of war but with the power of love.

Following Muslim tradition, Gandhi's body is cremated on a pyre as police try to keep onlookers from getting too close.

For Further Reading

Faber, Doris. *Mahatma Gandhi*. New York: Julian Messner, 1986.

Fischer, Louis. *Gandhi: His Life and Message for the World*. New York: Penguin Books, 1982.

Gandhi, Mahatma. *Gandhi: An Autobiography*. Boston: Beacon Press, 1957.

Gold, Gerald. *Gandhi: A Pictorial Biography*. New York: Newmarket Press, 1983.

Hunter, Nigel. *Gandhi*. New York: Brookwright Press, 1987.

Shirer, William. *Gandhi: A Memoir*. New York: Simon and Schuster, 1979.

The 1982 Academy Award winning film *Gandhi* starring Ben Kingsley also offers an excellent picture of the life of Mahatma Gandhi.

Index

About the Author

Caroline Evensen Lazo was born in Minneapolis, Minnesota. She spent much of her childhood visiting museums and attending plays written by her mother, Isobel Evensen, whose work earned national acclaim and became a lasting source of inspiration for her daughter.

Ms. Lazo attended the University of Oslo, Norway, and received a B.A. in Art History from the University of Minnesota. She has written extensively about art and architecture, and is the author of many books for young people, including *The Terra Cotta Army of Emperor Qin*, *Missing Treasure*, and *Endangered Species*.